Over-the-Hillisms

Over-the-Hillisms

What They Say
and What They Really Mean

CATHY HAMILTON

Andrews McMeel
Publishing

Kansas City

Over-the-Hillisms

04 05 06 07 08 TWP 10 9 8 7 6 5 4 3 2 1

ISBN: 0-7407-4743-6

Library of Congress Control Number: 2004101566

www.cathyhamilton.com

Book design by Holly Camerlinck

Attention: Schools and Businesses

Andrews McMeel books are available at quantity discounts with bulk purchase for educational, business, or sales promotional use. For information, please write to: Special Sales Department, Andrews McMeel Publishing, 4520 Main Street, Kansas City, Missouri 64111.

For Rex.
Over the hill we go!

"Now, in *my* day . . ."

Danger! Warning! When a senior opens with this phrase, you know you're going to hear another tired old story about the hardships of growing up in a different time, like walking five miles to school uphill both ways in the snow, living without speed dial, or having to actually get up from the sofa to change the channel on the TV.

"I'm having a senior moment."

Translation:

I've **forgotten** what I was talking about.
And to whom I was talking. In fact, I think
I've forgotten my own name. **Oh!**
I remember! Damn. Just lost it again.
Give me a minute. . . .

"Is that a boy or a girl?"

You know you're getting old when you lose the ability to distinguish between the sexes. When this starts happening, you would be well advised to eliminate the use of gender-specific titles like, "More coffee please, miss." You never know when that nice waitress will answer back, in a baritone voice: "Call me Fred. You want cream with that?"

"They just don't make 'em like they used to."

{ Usually used in reference to cars, houses, movies, and songs, this is *the* classic senior lament. }

Translation:

It's **hell** getting old.

"What is she *wearing*?"

This ism is typically used to comment on the more radical fashions of the day, including sheer tops, low-low-rise jeans, and extreme body piercings. Many seniors conveniently forget that this same ism was used by *their* elders to express disapproval of such shameful styles as flapper dresses, push-up bras, and stretch pants.

"Sex, sex, sex! That's all anybody ever thinks about anymore."

Translation:

I remember **sex**. It's all I used to think about. But now, what's the **point**?

"These kids today!"

You know you've crossed the threshold into middle age the moment you hear yourself utter these three words. Typically articulated with an air of disgust over the behavior of the younger generation, this ism's underlying meaning is "I'd give my eye teeth and half my 401(k) to be a kid again."

"What is this world coming to?!"

This is an oldster's standard reaction to hearing news of an event or trend that, in their mind, signals the end of the world as they know it. Examples include corporate scandals, gay marriage, and *Girls Gone Wild* videos.

"Oh, my Lord!"
(Or "Oh, my heavens!")

Old people have a tendency to summon the deity more frequently and with more urgency than their younger counterparts. Maybe this is because they perceive themselves to be in closer proximity to the pearly gates than they used to be and they want the deity to be intimately familiar with them when they arrive.

"Mercy me!/Have mercy!"

Just like their frequent tendency to summon the Most High, oldsters similarly enjoy asking for mercy at the drop of a hat. Mercy, in this case, often means pity, sympathy, or understanding, but it rarely means forgiveness as old people seldom have the energy to do anything wrong.

"Don't go to any trouble."

{ No self-respecting old person could sleep at night knowing people went to any extra effort to make them happy, comfortable, or well fed. There's way too much guilt involved in being the center of attention. }

"It's no trouble at all."

Now when someone says to the old person, "Don't go to any trouble," they're likely to hear the stock answer above. Even if Grandma is preparing a five-course meal from scratch with nothing but a hot plate, she'll never admit it was a big deal.

Translation:

Trouble? No trouble! Unless you call peeling **twenty** pounds of potatoes with arthritic hands, getting up at 4 a.m. to put the turkey in, and lugging SIX card tables and twenty-four folding chairs down from the attic "trouble." It was no trouble at **all**!

"You're skin and bones. Are you getting enough to eat?"

Heaven help the younger person who goes away to camp, college, or the military and loses a little weight around the middle. Now the older person will make it Priority One to fatten up the wayward child who is wasting away.

"Welcome to the club."

Old folks belong to lots of clubs. The Oh My Aching Back Club, the Too Tired to Care Club, the 39 and Holding Club, the I'm Paying an Obscene Amount of Money for Insurance and My Pharmacy Bill Is Still $400 a Month Club. And the ever-burgeoning My Worthless Kid Has Come Home to Live with Us Again Club.

Most folks use the above ism when they hear a younger person complain about something they've been dealing with for years.

"That's the way the cookie crumbles."

The crumbling cookie analogy, a relic used primarily by people over forty, usually refers to those "you win some, you lose some" scenarios, although it can be applied to amateur baking sessions.

"I'm not getting any younger, you know."

Here's one that's commonly uttered when an older woman gets tired of waiting indefinitely for something like a wedding, grandchildren, or her turn to use the telephone.

"I'm at my wits' end!"

Translation:

I am so **frustrated** over trying to program this damn VCR, I have lost my wits. I can no longer find anything **you** say or do witty, and I **seriously** doubt I will rediscover my wits in the next twenty-four hours. Everyone within **two** miles of me would do well to stay **clear** until my wits return, wherever they are.

"I'm getting too old for this."

This is what the skeptical senior says when, at a younger person's insistence, he climbs the ladder of the tree house to fetch an errant kite, embarks on a white-water rafting trip, or reluctantly joins in the "Bunny Hop" line at a family wedding.

"Now you listen to me, Buster (or Missy!)"

When an oldster addresses a male person as "Buster" or a female person as "Missy," the addressee should know this means one of two things:

The oldster is **angry** and really wants to get his point across, or

The geezer has completely **forgotten** whom he is addressing and "Buster" or "Missy" is the only proper name that comes immediately to mind.

"You're giving me gray hairs!"

Translation:

By constantly **worrying** about you,
day and night, I have **aged** at
four times the normal human rate
and am **now** the physiological
equivalent of my deceased grandmother.

"Turn it down!
I can't hear myself think!"

One of the many things kids don't understand is that when the music or TV is at high volume, it drowns out the inner monologue running through an elderly person's head, which, at any given time, goes something like this:

"Don't forget to defrost tonight's dinner. Did I take my medicine this morning? Put the wash in the dryer. What was the name of that book Oprah was talking about? Did I take my medicine at lunch? The toilet needs scrubbing. Is that a varicose vein? Remember to pick up the dry cleaning. What happened to the broom? Must schedule that mammogram. Is that a new hair? Who took all the Metamucil? How many pills am I supposed to have left?"

Old folks desperately need to hear this inner monologue or nothing will ever get done.

"Shoulda, woulda, coulda."

By the time most people reach their autumnal years, they will have identified more than five hundred things they should have, would have, or could have done, e.g.., gotten their master's degree, backpacked across Europe, auditioned for the Rockettes, had their tubes tied. That's why, when they hear a young whippersnapper voicing the same kind of regret, they answer back with the above ism . . . as if they've heard it all before.

"The older you get, the faster time flies."

{ Here's a little tidbit of truth warning us to make each second count, live each day as if it will be your last, stop and smell the roses . . . and all that other midlife crisis crap. }

"What's good enough for the goose is good enough for the gander."

{ This age-old ism, a proclamation of equality between the sexes dating back to pre-suffrage days, had feminist overtones before feminism was cool. When an old broad uses this one, say "Right on, sister!" }

"Let me tell you a little story . . ."

Uh-oh. When an elderly one opens with this ism, it means you're going to hear one of his special little fables, certain to conclude with an appropriate and instructive lesson. The moral of this *story* is likely to be no fun at all.

"See what you have to look forward to?"

Spoken with more than a touch of sarcasm, this ism warns the young of the more disturbing age-related body changes like varicose veins, foot bunions, hemorrhoids, male pattern baldness, and erectile dysfunction.

"Why, you're just a kid!"

This is what an oldster says when she asks a person how old he is and the answer is ten or more years younger than her respective age. It doesn't matter if the person is forty, fifty, or even seventy. If the number of years is less, that alone qualifies him for the "kid" designation.

"The classics never go out of style."

Here's a truism that tends to be taken to the extreme when one reaches old age. This one is an old geezer's attempt to justify his white bucks, lime green plaid shorts, and bowling shirt.

"Not now, my shows are on."

You know you've reached a certain age when you start referring to your favorite soap operas as "my shows." This is Stage One of a progressive disease called Serial Dependency Syndrome, in which victims start relating to soap characters as real people, talking back to them on the screen, and tuning out the world around them until the last cliffhanger of the day is through. The afflicted are relatively harmless, unless there is a cable outage in their neighborhood, at which time they will likely become violent.

"Turn down that racket!"

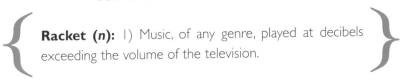

Racket (*n*): 1) Music, of any genre, played at decibels exceeding the volume of the television.

"I know exactly where I am."

{ A classic defense mechanism, this is what the old person says to persuade his passengers he's in control, even though it's taken an hour to complete a five-mile trip to Wal-Mart. }

Translation:

I **know** that we are somewhere between **home** and our final destination, and that's all **you** need to know at this time.

"They've changed it all around!"

You know you're getting older when it throws you for a gigantic loop to find your favorite store has changed the layout of their merchandise ... or when a restaurant changes their menu. This confuses an old person completely and they must take minutes, days, or even months to reorient themselves to the changes.

That's why, in department stores, you frequently hear older women crying out, in their loudest "emergency" voices: "What did you do with the Foundations department?" until a brigade of clerks rushes to their aid.

"Better talk to the wife* about that."

{ Here's another sure sign you're on the downhill side of the slope. When you start referring to the person you know most intimately in the world as "the wife" or "the old man," it means one of two things: }

1) You've entered Phase Three of the relationship, commonly called the "Marital Resignation Phase," or

2) You've completely forgotten his or her name.

*Substitute warden, ball and chain, boss, general, or old lady.

"What ever happened to 'Respect your elders'?"

Symptomatic of the so-called Rodney Dangerfield Syndrome, old folks say this when they feel like they "get no respect," which is approximately 95 percent of the time.

"What time does the Early Bird start?"

A sure sign you're getting long in the tooth is when, after decades of "dinner at eight," you suddenly become willing to eat dinner at 4:30 in the afternoon, whether you're hungry or not, just to save a couple bucks. What many early birds don't realize is that they almost always spend the money they saved on the food they buy at nine o'clock the same night, when ravenous hunger strikes and they head for the Piggly Wiggly in their house slippers.

"It's not an operation, it's a procedure."

Translation:

If I downplay the fact that I'm going in for **major** surgery by calling it a **procedure**, I'll feel **better** about the whole thing and people won't worry so much about me. On the **other** hand, I could call it what it is—**a quadruple bypass**—and milk the situation for all it's worth.

"Did I ever tell you about the time . . . ?"

(Or "Stop me if you've already heard this one . . .")

It's a known fact that the older you get, the more often you repeat yourself. The above ism, and its common alternative, are supposed to allow the listener an escape route if, in fact, the "walked-to-school-in-the-snow-uphill-both-ways" story has been repeated once, twice, or even ten times before.

"Is it hot (cold) in here?"

Another sign that you're getting on in years is when your body's temperature starts to run counter to everyone else's around you. This is especially true with menopausal women who are very likely to readjust the thermostat an average of seventeen times a day.

"That's a fancy pair of shoes you've got there."

What is it about old people and their fascination with shoes?! Don't they ever go to shoe stores anymore? Flashy cross-trainers with neon-colored Velcro fasteners and clear rubber soles are sure to garner the above observation, especially if they're on the feet of grandchildren. Young people don't understand this fascination, thinking shoes are—well, shoes. But compared to an old person's Rockport walkers, anything else seems over-the-top "fancy."

"Va, va, va, voom!"

Rule number one: Never take an old guy to a place like Hooters. After one beer, old guys tend to ignore their inner censors and actually verbalize out loud the thoughts going through their heads.

"Whoopsidaisies!"

It's a fact that, as people get older, they tend to lose the ability to control certain types of gaseous emissions. When an oldster lets one fly, as they say, you'll often hear the above ism as he or she feigns humiliation.

The truth is, they're not really embarrassed. They've reverted to the childhood pleasure of letting one rip and getting away with it.

"A little respect . . . ?"

This is what an oldster says when the younger people in the room are talking about his personality flaws as if he were actually not standing there . . . in his skivvies.

"Now I've heard everything!"

Here's another common middle-aged reaction to hearing of developments in the world that, in another day and age, would be downright shocking, ridiculously unlikely, or physically impossible. Examples include sheep cloning, professional women's basketball, and Viagra.

"Man, has *he* aged!"

This is what an over-the-hillster says when you see an old movie star who has been out of the public eye for a decade or so. The irony here is that the movie star is probably older than you are and has had several plastic surgeries, to boot! In this context, think of how much older *you* must look!

"I haven't seen you in a coon's age."

The average life expectancy of a raccoon is 3.5 years, with an absolute maximum of 13. (And that's if the raccoon is a nonsmoker who exercises daily.) Thus, the above ism can be translated as follows:

I haven't seen you in approximately three and a half years but it could be as many as thirteen. I would have to know the condition and lifestyle of the animal involved.

"She's been nipped and tucked more times than Joan Rivers*."

{ Here's a typical reaction to seeing a Hollywood celebrity whose eyebrow lift or boob job is glaringly obvious. It is usually uttered with more than a smidgen of envy. }

Translation:

Damn. Why can't **face-lifts** be **covered** by my medical plan?

*Substitute any celebrity symbol of plastic surgery excess.

"Are you done with the obits page?"

Another definite sign you're coasting rapidly down the mountain is when you open your morning newspaper, pass up the headlines, and go directly to the obituary page, where you scan for familiar names.

"What was I *thinking*?"

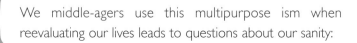

We middle-agers use this multipurpose ism when reevaluating our lives leads to questions about our sanity:

- When we browse through photographs of ourselves wearing those enormous shoulder pads from the '80s

- When we purchased that time-share in Haiti because it was a "really good deal"

- When we had one too many martinis at the Wayne Newton show in Vegas and ended up in the Little Chapel on the Strip with a waiter named Raoul

It's also what we say when we just don't remember what we were thinking.

"You're probably too young to remember . . ."

For as hard as they try to not look or act it, middle-aged folks are always saying things to reveal how old they are. This ism is a perfect example. This is how the oldster prefaces one of those nostalgic stories of when bikinis actually covered a woman's buns or milk was delivered to the back door in glass bottles by men dressed in white.

"That was before you were born."

Here's yet another example of how old folks feel compelled to remind others of their age. Some folks say it so often, with so much authority, that their grandchildren come to believe they were present for Lee's surrender at Appomattox or the fall of the Roman Empire.

"Now, where did I park?"

Venture out into any sprawling parking lot or garage and you're likely to see a smattering of red rubber balls, rabbit's feet, and other bright-colored objects affixed to various antennae. These are the antennae of absentminded over-the-hillsters who have a tendency to forget where they parked.

The rest of them are
wandering around, keys in hand,
muttering the above question.

"Ooofff."

This is the sound an old fogey makes when he sinks into a chair that's a little too deep or low to the ground. He will inevitably sit in such a chair for hours upon hours, all because he's afraid he's unable to get up again. Eventually, though, nature calls or bedtime arrives, and he's forced to go for it, at which time he's likely to emit the following sound . . .

"Arrrrgh!"

Interchangeable with "grrraaah!" and "hummmnfff," this is the sound the fogey makes when he tries to elevate himself from that same chair. Studies have shown that the louder you groan, the better your chances of a successful lift-off. It the same principle as those Olympic weight lifters, the ones who yell from the bellows of their gut when they perform the clean and jerk.

"What's wrong with what I'm wearing?"

Another sure sign of getting old is not giving a damn what you look like in your high-waisted Haggar slacks and "Old Fart" T-shirt.

"Give me some skin."

Predating "Give me five" or its more contemporary counterpart "Gimme some," this is one of many expressions that will date an over-the-hillster faster than the support hose on their feet. Additional examples include "Hey, Daddy-O," "You're the bee's knees," and "Groovy, man."

"It's about yay big."

You know you're getting on in years when the only way you can accurately illustrate the physical proportions of something is by saying "yay big." "Yay" is an inexact term meaning "just about so" or "something around that there." It is commonly used to describe newborn grandchildren and fish that got away.

"This, too, shall pass."

{ An old standby, these feeble words of comfort are used when the oldster can't remember any other bits of sage advice. }

Translation:

I can't **remember** any other bits of **sage** advice, so I'm using this old **standby**. Feeble words of comfort, eh?

"C'mon over here and let me get a good look at you."

Woe to the poor youngster who hears this summons from an elder person. This ism should be a warning that cheek pinching, nose tweaking, hair mussing, and crushing body hugs are in his or her immediate future.

"My body's got a mind of its own."

Translation:

I'm **sucking** in my **stomach** with all my **might** and still can't see my **feet**. What's **up** with that?

"I may be old but I'm not dead."

When an old guy is busted by his wife for ogling a busty young woman as she walks down the street, he will often resort to this defensive claim. The idea here is to remind said wife that he is, in fact, knocking on death's door and she should at least allow him these last guilty pleasures.

It rarely works.

"What kind of a contraption is that?"

Another sure sign you're descending the south side of the hill is that you start using words like "contraption" or "new-fangled" to describe common household appliances like VCRs, coffee bean grinders, and Palm Pilots.

"Contraption" is only the start.
Soon, your vocabulary will be peppered
with such chestnuts as "whippersnapper,"
"scalawag," and "by-cracky," and
pretty soon nobody will know
what the hell you're talking about.

"I remember when a tank of gas cost five dollars*."

There are few things more gripe-worthy to an over-the-hillster than the increasing price of gas, unless you count the increasing price of a loaf of bread, a gallon of milk, or movie tickets.

Oldsters are fascinated with monitoring the price at the pump, noting every two cent per gallon increase or decline in price, announcing it to their families in a daily report:

"Pump 'N' Stump's unleaded is $2.05. I remember when a tank of gas cost 22 cents."

*Amount will vary depending on age of oldster and his make of car.

"You only live once."

After years of frugal, guarded, and responsible behavior, sometimes an oldster gets the urge to throw caution to the wind and do something reckless, like skydiving, bungee jumping, or mud wrestling at the local strip club. The above ism is his rationalization for such craziness.

Translation:

Talk me OUt of it ... please!!!

"Put another album on the hi-fi."

You know you're truly on the downside of the hill when you own a CD collection numbering in the hundreds and a stereo system worth $3,000, and you refer to them as "albums" and the "hi-fi."

"I'm seventy* years young."

This is the over-the-hillster attempting to convince himself and others that the numeral corresponding with the number of years lived is actually an indicator of youth rather than age.

Who are you kidding with this one?

*Substitute any age over forty.

"My get up and go just got up and went."

This is an oldster's attempt at using humor to deflect attention from the fact that a trip to the mall has rendered her useless for the next three days.

"Here, read this!"

This is what he says as he passes the menu, phone book, or theater program to the younger person next to him. Oldsters learn it is often quicker and easier to delegate the task of reading the fine print than to rummage around for the reading glasses, adjust the lighting, and slowly squint their eyes until the focus is just right.

"Does this come in the large-print edition?"

Translation:

I've **exhausted** the strongest pair of reading **glasses** I can buy and, for some reason, they don't have *Contract Bridge for Dummies* in Books on Tape.

"You can't take it with you."

This is what old folks commonly say as they're gleefully spending their retirement fund on big-ticket items like recreational vehicles and cruises. It doesn't come as music to the ears of offspring hoping to reap the rewards of their parents' nest egg, particularly when Mom and Dad are saying it while wearing "We're Spending Our Kids' Inheritance" T-shirts.

"You call that music?
I call it noise."

Don't even try to explain the musicality of rhythmically scratching a record back and forth to an old person. They remember that sound as being a sure sign that someone has ruined their Barry Manilow album.

"Has anyone seen my glasses?"

{ Next to bingo and golf, hunting for eyeglasses is the most popular pastime of everyone over the age of forty. The hunt for glasses is like the U.S. mail: It never ends. }

The above ism is often asked while the oldster is wearing his specs on top of his head, around his neck, or, occasionally, on the bridge of his nose, where they belong.

"Where'd I put my keys?"

Next to bingo, golf, and hunting for eyeglasses, the most popular pastime for everyone over forty is hunting for their keys. This question is frequently posed by older women while rummaging through the dark depths of their handbags. Extra care should be used to check door locks, ignitions, coat pockets, and the top of the car before asking this question aloud.

"Would you be a dear and . . . ?"

Gerontologists aren't sure exactly when the word "dear" creeps into the vocabulary of the middle-aged but studies have shown it begins somewhere between the ages of forty-nine and fifty-four.

This ism is a particularly effective way of garnering a favor from a younger person because to deny the request would signal that the person is not a "dear" and everyone desires, deeply and at their core, to be dear.

"Give me a hand, will you?"

To a younger person, on the surface this ism appears to be a straightforward request for assistance, like "Help me lift this heavy object" or "Hold the ladder while I climb up and change the lightbulb."

But when a senior says "Give me a hand, will you?" what he really means is "How's about *you* do the work and I just watch?"

"My, how you've grown!"

{ Oldsters love this one, typically used to comment on the development of a grandchild, niece, or nephew. }

Translation:

Either you've gotten a **lot** taller since last I saw you or I am shrinking at a much **faster** rate than I thought.

"What did I come in here for?"

Another sure sign you're on the downward slope is when you walk into the kitchen or bedroom and can't remember what you're doing there. This is a universal phenomenon that causes oldsters to pad around the house in circles, scratching their heads until the mystery is solved. This can take hours, sometimes days.

The record is held by Marian B. Skeener, who paced 4,089 laps around her condo for nine days until she remembered she was only going after a needle and thread.

"Where'd this hair come from?"

One of the misadventures of old age is discovering hair in places you never knew could produce follicles. When it comes to degrees of wonder, the aging body's increasing ability to sprout whiskers in unexpected places is second only to its unusual capacity for gaseous emissions.

"Cold hands, warm heart."

Here's a charming little expression that means "Sure, the circulation in my hands is virtually nonexistent but at least I have a charming little expression about it!"

"They're not wrinkles, they're character lines."

Ah, the endless joys of denial! By calling wrinkles "character lines," liver spots "freckles," or gray hair "silver highlights," we transport ourselves into the wonderful world of "what we don't admit won't depress us."

"Just wait until you're my age."

These are some of the most ominous words an old person can say to a younger person.

Such forewarnings prompt visuals
of sagging flesh, thinning hair,
liver spots, and progressive dementia
causing the younger person to respond
half-heartedly, "I can't wait."

"I'm thirty-nine and holding."

Here's a classic dodge of the "How old are you?" question. "Holding" in this case can mean "holding onto dear life," "holding my stomach in," or "holding fast to that ridiculous thirty-nine fantasy."

"Pull my finger."

As disgusting as this ritual is, when an old geezer is in "pull my finger" mode, refusing to cooperate is futile. There's a natural sense of urgency in the "pull my finger" request. An old fogey will be very insistent ("Pull my finger. Go ahead, pull it! Hurry!") until you relent.

The payoff will prove tasteless to some, but then, who are we to deprive our elders of a bit of joy once in a while?

"In my day, people actually held each other when they danced."

There's no doubt about it. Ballroom dancing is fast becoming a lost art, which can be a depressing thought for the oldster who pines nostalgically for the good old days on the dance floor.

That's why people of a certain age should never be allowed to watch MTV, which gives new meaning to the term "dancing cheek to cheek."

"Pass me my cheaters, will you?"

Cheaters *(n)*: Reading glasses, magnifying glasses, readers. Available in varying powers of magnification. Mandatory equipment for those who have crossed over to the old side. Frequently found in multiples in the home, sometimes more than one to a room, as they are easily misplaced.

"Damn doctors,
they don't know anything."

A pretty sure sign you've crested the hill is when doctors, lawyers, and politicians become "damn doctors," "damn lawyers," and "damn politicians," and none of them know anything anymore.

The "damn doctor" referred to in this ism probably just kept you waiting for an hour and a half, only to tell you that you need to lose that gut and send you home without any Viagra samples.

"A lady never tells her age."

One of the best excuses for a woman not to reveal her biological age, this ism is accepted in most situations except the doctor's office, the DMV, and Willard Scott's *Today* show list of centurions.

"Okeedokee."

The older you get, the more you seem to appreciate a silly rhyme. That's why expressions such as "Okeedokee," "Super Duper," "Easy Peasy," "Loosey Goosey," and the ever-popular "Ready, Freddy?" are beloved by over-the-hillsters everywhere.

"Okeedokee" is simply an old person's way of saying "fine with me" or "okay," but with the rhyme factored in and those extra syllables that seem to roll off the tongue, it tends to come out more like a jingle than an actual word.

"I'm old enough to know better."

Here's another one of those stock answers to the question "How old are you?" Obviously an attempt to evade the question, it can be substituted with "Old enough to know you never ask an older person her age" or "Old enough, thank you."

"I've got one foot in the grave."

A melodramatic exaggeration used by an old one to foster sympathy from those around him, this ism can mean anything from "My cholesterol's high" to "I think my hemorrhoids are back."

"Don't be a stranger."

{ Although this is normally translated to mean "I'd love to see you again soon," sometimes what the over-the-hillster really means is "I sure hope I recognize you the next time we run into each other." }

"I don't understand."

These three little words eventually become the oldster's stock answer to just about everything, including new tax regulations, instruction manuals, anything having to do with computers, and Comedy Central.

"In dog years, I'd be dead."

{ This ism seems to be a misguided attempt to reassure yourself that you're not as old as all that by comparing your age to the canine life cycle. True, a forty-five-year-old is the equivalent of 315 in dog years, but does getting the best of a cocker spaniel *really* make you feel better? }

"You remind me of someone."

An American poet, Ogden Nash, observed, "Middle age is when you've met so many people that every new person you meet reminds you of someone else." That's why older folks are constantly using the above ism when they encounter a new face.

The problem arises, of course, when the elder in question meets a person who reminds him of—say—his sister Esther, only to be reminded that it is Esther herself who is shaking his hand.

"Gravity sure takes its toll."

{ This is another way of saying "My boobs are somewhere around my waist and my butt has fallen to my knees and it's all Isaac Newton's fault." }

"My back goes out more than I do."

{ This isn't so much an expression as a statement of fact. }

You know you're getting up there in years when you go to the chiropractor more often than you go to the movies.

"Must be the old 'Arthur-itis' acting up again."

Oldsters love to give their physical ailments cute little nicknames. Perhaps it's because medical conditions are easier to live with when reduced to cutesy monikers like "rheumatiz," "Arthur-itis," "a hitch in my get-along," or "Montezuma's Revenge."

"Don't get your knickers in a knot (or panties in a twist)."

{ Interpreted to mean "don't worry" or, in the modern vernacular, "chill," these idiomatic expressions are heard only from the *really* old. }

"Huh?"

The older you get, the more you'll be repeating this ism, which simply means "Please speak up. I didn't hear what you just said." When you get a *lot* older, your "Huh?"'s become progressively louder until, finally, you are screaming with a panicky expression on your face. (At this point, it sounds more like "Heh?") People who make a practice of talking to oldsters should be advised that the volume at which a "Huh?" is uttered is the volume at which their statement should be repeated. **Just a good rule of thumb.**

"You're only as old as you feel."

{ Here's a truism that makes the point that a forty-year-old couch potato who gets winded climbing the stairs is no better off than the sixty-year-old who runs three miles a day and goes out dancing at night. }

Groucho Marx added his own twist to this ism when he said, "A man is only as old as the woman he feels."

"Do you feel a draft?"

What used to be called "ventilation" is now called a "draft." The world is a drafty place for the over-the-hillster. Seniors find these bothersome breezes in cars, planes, movie theaters, restaurants, church, doctor's offices, even their own homes . . . anywhere there's a functioning fan or heating and cooling system in operation.

"If I've told you once, I've told you a thousand times!"

{ Old people have a tendency to exaggerate. It probably wasn't a thousand times. It was more like a hundred times. They've just lost count. }

"That's what's wrong with this generation . . ."

{ This ism is a standard complaint about younger folks' slacker mentality, left-leaning politics, or lack of moral turpitude. }

The older generation is never satisfied with the performance of the younger, even though history always proves that each generation, seen as shiftless in the eyes of their elders, grows up to become capable and productive members of society who, in turn, complain about the generation behind them.

"Old age is a state of mind."

Translation:

If you *think* you're young,
you *are* young. So what if the
candles on your **birthday** cake
have set off the smoke detectors?

"It seems like only yesterday . . ."

Here's a bittersweet prologue to any story illustrating how quickly time has flown for the over-the-hillster. Examples include:

It seems like only **yesterday** I was **walking** down the aisle.

It seems like only **yesterday** we were **bringing** you home from the **hospital**.

It **seems** like only yesterday I had only **ONE** chin.